Discovering the Industrial Landscape: An Introduction to Industrial Archaeology for Students

Grace Taylor

Copyright © [2023]

Title: Discovering the Industrial Landscape: An Introduction to Industrial Archaeology for Students

Author's: Grace Taylor.

All rights reserved. No part of this publication may be reproduced, stored in a retrieval system, or transmitted in any form or by any means, electronic, mechanical, photocopying, recording, or otherwise, without the prior written permission of the publisher or author, except in the case of brief quotations embodied in critical reviews and certain other non-commercial uses permitted by copyright law.

This book was printed and published by [Publisher's: Grace Taylor]   in [2023]

ISBN:

TABLE OF CONTENTS

Recapitulation of Key Concepts and Themes

Implications and Significance of Industrial Archaeology for Students

Encouraging Further Exploration of Industrial Archaeology

Chapter 1: Introduction to Industrial Archaeology

Definition and Scope of Industrial Archaeology

Industrial archaeology is a fascinating field that focuses on studying and understanding the material remains of past industrial activities. It provides valuable insights into the development of industries, technological advancements, and their impact on society. In this subchapter, we will explore the definition and scope of industrial archaeology, aiming to provide students with a comprehensive understanding of this specialized branch of archaeology.

Industrial archaeology can be defined as the branch of archaeology that deals with the investigation, recording, and interpretation of industrial sites, structures, artifacts, and landscapes. It involves the study of various industries, including mining, manufacturing, transportation, and energy production, among others. Through careful analysis of these remains, industrial archaeologists strive to reconstruct the processes, working conditions, and social dynamics of past industrial societies.

The scope of industrial archaeology is diverse and encompasses a wide range of activities. It involves fieldwork, archival research, artifact analysis, and documentation. Fieldwork often includes surveys and excavations of industrial sites, where archaeologists carefully excavate and record the stratigraphy and material culture. This data is then analyzed and interpreted to provide a comprehensive understanding of the site and its historical context.

Archival research is another crucial aspect of industrial archaeology. By studying historical documents, maps, photographs, and oral histories, researchers can gain insights into how industries operated, the technological innovations employed, and the social and economic impact of industrialization. This interdisciplinary approach allows students to delve into the complexities of industrial societies and the factors that shaped them.

Industrial archaeology also involves the analysis of artifacts and structures. Artifacts recovered from industrial sites can provide valuable information about production techniques, working conditions, and the everyday lives of workers. Structures, such as mills, factories, and warehouses, offer insights into architectural design, machinery layout, and the organization of industrial spaces.

Furthermore, industrial archaeology extends beyond physical remains. It includes the study of industrial landscapes, such as canals, railways, and mines, which played an integral role in shaping the industrial world. Understanding the relationship between these landscapes and their social and economic contexts is essential for comprehending the full impact of industrialization on society.

In conclusion, industrial archaeology is a multidisciplinary field that provides a unique perspective on the history of industrialization. By studying the material remains of past industries, students gain insights into technological advancements, social dynamics, and the environmental impact of industrial activities. This subchapter aims to introduce students to the definition and scope of industrial archaeology, encouraging them to explore this fascinating field further.

Importance of Industrial Archaeology

The Importance of Industrial Archaeology

Industrial archaeology is a fascinating field that offers students a unique opportunity to delve into the past and understand the development of human civilization through the lens of industry. It is an interdisciplinary subject that combines elements of history, archaeology, engineering, and architecture to study the physical remains of industrial activities and their impact on society. In this subchapter, we will explore the significance of industrial archaeology and how it contributes to our understanding of the industrial landscape.

One of the key reasons why industrial archaeology is important is that it sheds light on the technological advancements and innovations that have shaped our world. By studying the remains of factories, mills, mines, and other industrial sites, students can gain insight into the tools, machinery, and processes that were crucial in driving economic growth and social transformation. This knowledge is invaluable in understanding the evolution of industries and their impact on human society.

Furthermore, industrial archaeology provides a tangible link to our industrial heritage. It allows students to explore the physical remnants of our past, such as factories and industrial buildings, which are often neglected or demolished in favor of modern development. By studying these structures, students can gain an understanding of the social, economic, and cultural context in which they were built and used. This knowledge helps us preserve our industrial heritage and appreciate the contributions made by those who came before us.

Industrial archaeology also plays a crucial role in urban planning and heritage management. By studying the industrial landscape, students can contribute to the identification and preservation of historically significant sites. This knowledge is essential for making informed decisions about conservation, restoration, and adaptive reuse of industrial structures. It ensures that our industrial heritage is not lost to the ravages of time and provides a foundation for sustainable development in industrial areas.

Moreover, industrial archaeology encourages a critical analysis of the negative impacts of industry on the environment and society. By studying the remnants of industrial pollution, such as mining waste or factory effluents, students can gain an understanding of the long-term consequences of industrial activities. This knowledge is crucial in developing strategies for environmental remediation and sustainable industrial practices.

In conclusion, industrial archaeology is a vital field of study for students interested in archaeology and related disciplines. It offers a unique perspective on the development of human society and provides insights into technological advancements, urban planning, heritage preservation, and environmental sustainability. By exploring the industrial landscape, students can gain a deeper understanding of our past and contribute to shaping a better future.

Evolution of Industrial Archaeology as a Field of Study

Industrial archaeology, as a field of study, has experienced a remarkable evolution over the years. In the book "Discovering the Industrial Landscape: An Introduction to Industrial Archaeology for Students," we delve into the fascinating journey of this discipline, addressing the interests of students with a passion for archaeology.

Industrial archaeology emerged in the mid-20th century as a response to the rapid transformation of societies due to industrialization. With the advent of the Industrial Revolution, traditional agricultural communities transitioned into bustling urban centers, leaving behind a rich tapestry of industrial remains. Recognizing the need to document and interpret these remnants, archaeologists began exploring factories, mills, mines, and other industrial sites.

Initially, the focus of industrial archaeology was primarily on the material culture and structures associated with industries. However, as the field progressed, it expanded to encompass a broader range of interdisciplinary approaches, incorporating historical, social, and economic perspectives. This multidisciplinary approach allowed researchers to gain a deeper understanding of the impact of industrialization on society and the environment.

One of the key milestones in the evolution of industrial archaeology was the recognition of the importance of preserving industrial heritage. As industries became obsolete and faced demolition, efforts were made to protect and conserve significant sites. This shift in mindset led to the establishment of industrial museums and heritage centers, where artifacts and machinery were displayed, and the stories of industrial communities were brought to life.

Another significant development in the field was the utilization of new technologies. Industrial archaeologists started employing advanced surveying techniques, such as LiDAR and aerial photography, to uncover hidden industrial landscapes. Moreover, digital tools enabled the creation of virtual reconstructions, allowing students and researchers to experience industrial sites that no longer exist.

Furthermore, the scope of industrial archaeology widened to include the study of industrial landscapes, considering the spatial relationships between various industrial elements. This approach emphasized the interconnectedness of factories, transportation networks, and workers' settlements, providing insights into the social dynamics of industrial communities.

In conclusion, the field of industrial archaeology has evolved from a study of material remains to a multidisciplinary exploration of industrial landscapes and their societal implications. "Discovering the Industrial Landscape: An Introduction to Industrial Archaeology for Students" aims to captivate students interested in archaeology by introducing them to this fascinating field. By understanding the evolution of industrial archaeology, students can appreciate the significance of industrial heritage and contribute to its preservation for future generations.

Careers in Industrial Archaeology

As students with a passion for archaeology, you may find yourselves drawn to the fascinating field of industrial archaeology. This subchapter aims to shed light on the diverse career opportunities available within this niche, offering you a glimpse into the world of uncovering the past through the remnants of industry.

Industrial archaeology examines the material remains of industrial activities from the past, including factories, mills, canals, railways, and mines. It provides invaluable insights into how societies functioned and evolved, offering a unique perspective on the development of technology, labor, and the impact of industry on the environment.

One prominent career path for aspiring industrial archaeologists is that of a heritage consultant. Heritage consultants work closely with government agencies, private organizations, and communities to preserve and manage industrial sites. This role involves conducting surveys, documenting historical structures, and advising on conservation and restoration projects. By combining your archaeological expertise with an understanding of heritage legislation and policy, you can contribute to the preservation of our industrial past.

Another exciting avenue in industrial archaeology is becoming a field archaeologist. Field archaeologists work on excavation sites, uncovering and analyzing artifacts, structures, and landscapes. In the context of industrial archaeology, this could involve excavating a disused mine or a forgotten railway station. This hands-on work allows you to directly engage with the physical remnants of industry and gain a deeper understanding of the past.

For those with a passion for research and academia, pursuing a career as an industrial archaeologist in universities or research institutions might be the ideal choice. This path involves conducting in-depth studies, publishing research papers, and contributing to the scholarly understanding of industrial history. You may specialize in a particular aspect, such as the impact of industrialization on local communities or the technological advancements of a specific industry.

Other potential careers include museum curators, historical interpreters, and cultural resource managers, where you can utilize your knowledge of industrial archaeology to educate and engage the public.

In conclusion, the field of industrial archaeology offers an array of exciting career prospects for students passionate about archaeology. Whether you choose to work in heritage management, field excavation, research, or public outreach, your expertise in industrial archaeology will contribute to uncovering and preserving our industrial heritage for future generations. Embrace the opportunity to explore the remnants of the past and embark on a fulfilling career in industrial archaeology.

Chapter 2: The Industrial Revolution and its Impact

Origins and Spread of the Industrial Revolution

The Industrial Revolution was a transformative period in human history that brought about significant changes in the way we live, work, and interact. It marked the transition from an agrarian and handicraft-based economy to one dominated by industrial production and machinery. This subchapter will delve into the origins and spread of this revolution, shedding light on its impact on society, economy, and the archaeological remains that can help us understand this fascinating period.

The Industrial Revolution originated in 18th-century Britain, spurred by a combination of factors. One key factor was the availability of abundant natural resources, including coal and iron ore, which were crucial for the development of new manufacturing processes. Additionally, Britain had a stable political and legal system that encouraged entrepreneurship and innovation. Technological advancements, such as the invention of the steam engine by James Watt, also played a vital role in driving industrialization.

As the Industrial Revolution took hold in Britain, it gradually spread to other parts of Europe and North America. This subchapter will explore the various factors that led to the diffusion of industrialization, including trade networks, colonialism, and the exchange of ideas through scientific societies and publications. It will highlight how the spread of industrialization varied across different regions, with some areas embracing it more rapidly than others.

To understand the impact of the Industrial Revolution, it is essential to examine the archaeological remains it left behind. Industrial archaeology is a discipline that focuses on studying the material evidence of industrialization, including factories, mines, canals, and workers' housing. By analyzing these remains, archaeologists can gain insights into the working conditions, technological advancements, and social dynamics of the time.

Furthermore, this subchapter will discuss the importance of industrial heritage preservation. As industrial landscapes continue to be transformed or demolished, it becomes crucial to document and protect these sites for future generations. Students interested in archaeology can play a vital role in this process by learning about industrial heritage management and advocating for its preservation.

In conclusion, the origins and spread of the Industrial Revolution are fascinating topics that shed light on the profound changes brought about by this period. Through the study of archaeology, students can gain a deeper understanding of the societal, economic, and technological transformations that took place and the role industrial heritage preservation plays in ensuring the legacy of this remarkable era.

Key Inventions and Technological Advancements

In the fascinating world of industrial archaeology, the study of key inventions and technological advancements is crucial to understanding the evolution of human civilization and the industrial landscape. This subchapter will delve into some of the most significant innovations that have shaped our modern world, providing students with a comprehensive overview of the milestones achieved throughout history.

One of the most groundbreaking inventions in human history was the steam engine, which played a pivotal role in the Industrial Revolution. Developed by James Watt in the 18th century, the steam engine revolutionized transportation, manufacturing, and agriculture. It paved the way for the creation of steam-powered locomotives, factories, and agricultural machinery, transforming the world as we knew it.

Another crucial technological advancement was the Bessemer process, introduced by Henry Bessemer in the mid-19th century. This process revolutionized steel production by allowing for the mass production of high-quality steel at a significantly reduced cost. The Bessemer process enabled the construction of massive structures like skyscrapers and bridges, thereby shaping urban landscapes across the globe.

The invention of the assembly line by Henry Ford in the early 20th century also had a profound impact on industrialization. This innovative production method allowed for the mass production of automobiles, making them more affordable and accessible to the general public. The assembly line not only transformed the automotive industry but also influenced manufacturing processes in various sectors, accelerating industrialization worldwide.

Advancements in communication technology also played a crucial role in shaping the industrial landscape. The invention of the telegraph by Samuel Morse in the early 19th century revolutionized long-distance communication. This groundbreaking invention paved the way for the development of the telephone and eventually led to the birth of the internet, connecting people and industries across the globe.

These are just a few examples of the key inventions and technological advancements that have shaped our industrial landscape. By studying and understanding these milestones, students of industrial archaeology gain a deeper appreciation for the rich history of human innovation and its impact on our physical surroundings. Furthermore, exploring these advancements provides valuable insights into the social, economic, and environmental changes brought about by industrialization. As future archaeologists, it is essential to grasp the significance of these inventions and their lasting legacy in order to preserve and interpret industrial heritage for generations to come.

Social and Economic Effects of the Industrial Revolution

Title: Social and Economic Effects of the Industrial Revolution

Introduction:
The Industrial Revolution, a period of rapid industrialization that took place from the late 18th to the early 19th century, had profound social and economic effects on society. In this subchapter, we will explore the transformative impact of this era on various aspects of life, focusing on the social and economic changes that unfolded during this time.

Social   Effects:
One of the most significant social effects of the Industrial Revolution was the urbanization of society. As factories emerged and industries grew, people migrated from rural areas to cities in search of employment opportunities. This mass migration led to the formation of crowded urban centers, giving rise to new social structures and challenges. The growth of cities also brought about the development of slums and poor living conditions for the working class, leading to social unrest and the rise of labor movements.

Furthermore, the Industrial Revolution brought changes in family dynamics. As more women and children entered the workforce, traditional gender roles were challenged. The separation of work and home life became more pronounced, as families struggled to adapt to the demands of industrial labor.

Economic   Effects:
The Industrial Revolution marked a shift from an agrarian economy to a manufacturing-based one. New technologies and machines revolutionized production methods, leading to increased productivity

and the growth of industries such as textiles, iron, and coal. This surge in production not only fueled economic growth but also led to a rise in capitalism and the accumulation of wealth among industrialists.

The Industrial Revolution also had a profound impact on the global economy. As European nations embraced industrialization, they began to dominate global trade and establish colonies to secure resources and markets. This economic expansion laid the foundation for the modern global economy and set the stage for the rise of capitalism.

Conclusion:
The social and economic effects of the Industrial Revolution were far-reaching and continue to shape our world today. From the massive urbanization and migration of people to the changing dynamics of family life, the Industrial Revolution transformed societies in profound ways. Simultaneously, the shift to a manufacturing-based economy and the rise of capitalism reshaped the global economic landscape. Understanding these effects is crucial to comprehending the origins and consequences of industrialization, providing valuable insights into our current industrial landscape.

As students of archaeology, studying the Industrial Revolution enables us to uncover the material remains of this transformative era. By examining industrial sites, artifacts, and historical records, we can gain a deeper understanding of the social and economic changes that unfolded during this pivotal period in human history.

Transformation of Industrial Landscapes

Industrial landscapes have undergone significant transformations over the years, leaving behind a rich legacy of history and artifacts. This subchapter aims to introduce students to the fascinating field of industrial archaeology and explore the various ways in which industrial landscapes have evolved.

The process of industrialization brought about a radical change in the physical environment, as natural landscapes were reshaped to accommodate factories, mines, canals, and railroads. The transformation of these landscapes is a testament to human ingenuity and the impact of industrialization on society.

One of the most noticeable transformations in industrial landscapes is the construction of factories. These structures, often massive and imposing, were designed to house machinery and accommodate large-scale production. Students will learn about the architectural features of factories, such as their distinctive chimneys and large windows, which provided ample light for workers.

Mining landscapes also underwent significant changes as mining operations expanded. As students delve into this topic, they will discover the traces left behind by mining activities, such as spoil heaps, mine entrances, and machinery. These remnants provide valuable insights into the techniques and technologies employed in the extraction of minerals.

Transportation networks played a crucial role in the industrial revolution, bringing raw materials to factories and finished goods to markets. Students will explore the transformation of landscapes through the construction of canals, railways, and roads. They will learn about the engineering challenges faced during the creation of these networks and how they impacted the movement of goods and people.

The subchapter will also delve into the social aspects of industrial landscapes. Students will study the impact of industrialization on the lives of workers, including the creation of company towns and the development of housing for workers. They will gain an understanding of the living conditions, social structures, and labor struggles that characterized these communities.

Furthermore, students will be introduced to the concept of industrial heritage and the importance of preserving industrial landscapes. They will learn about the efforts made by archaeologists, historians, and preservationists to protect and interpret these sites for future generations.

By exploring the transformation of industrial landscapes, students will develop a deeper appreciation for the significance of industrial archaeology. They will gain insight into the interconnectedness of society, technology, and the environment, and understand the role of industrial landscapes in shaping our modern world.

Chapter 3: Methodology of Industrial Archaeology

Surveying and Mapping Industrial Sites

In the field of industrial archaeology, surveying and mapping play a crucial role in understanding and documenting the industrial landscape. By employing a range of techniques and tools, archaeologists can effectively study, record, and interpret industrial sites. This subchapter aims to introduce students to the fundamentals of surveying and mapping in industrial archaeology.

Industrial sites encompass a wide range of structures and features, including factories, mills, mines, and transportation infrastructure. These sites often span vast areas and require systematic surveying to accurately document their layout and characteristics. Surveying techniques include both traditional methods, such as measuring distances and angles using theodolites and tape measures, as well as modern technologies like total stations and GPS. Students will learn how to use these tools and techniques to create accurate maps and plans of industrial sites.

Mapping industrial sites involves capturing spatial data and presenting it in a visual format. Maps serve as valuable tools for recording and analyzing the distribution and arrangement of buildings, machinery, and other features within a site. Students will explore different types of maps commonly used in industrial archaeology, such as topographic maps, plans, and sections. They will also learn how to utilize computer software, such as Geographic Information Systems (GIS), to create digital maps and perform spatial analysis.

The subchapter will delve into the importance of surveying and mapping in industrial archaeology. Students will discover how these techniques help archaeologists identify patterns, understand the layout and function of industrial sites, and reconstruct their historical development. They will also explore how surveying and mapping contribute to the conservation and management of industrial heritage.

Furthermore, the subchapter will address the challenges and ethical considerations that arise when surveying and mapping industrial sites. Students will learn about the importance of obtaining permissions, respecting private property, and adhering to ethical guidelines during fieldwork. They will also explore how environmental factors, such as vegetation and weathering, can affect surveying and mapping efforts.

By the end of this subchapter, students will have a solid foundation in the principles and practices of surveying and mapping industrial sites. They will understand the significance of these techniques in industrial archaeology and gain the skills necessary to conduct their own surveys and create accurate maps.

Excavation Techniques and Strategies

In the fascinating world of industrial archaeology, the excavation process plays a crucial role in uncovering the hidden stories of the past. Excavation techniques and strategies are essential tools for students of archaeology who are determined to explore the industrial landscape. This subchapter will introduce you to the key considerations and methods employed in excavating industrial sites, providing you with a solid foundation for your future fieldwork endeavors.

Before diving into the specifics, it is important to understand the significance of excavation in industrial archaeology. Unlike traditional archaeological sites, industrial sites often present unique challenges due to their size, complexity, and the presence of potentially hazardous materials. As a result, careful planning and execution are required to ensure the safety of the archaeological team and the preservation of important artifacts and structures.

One crucial aspect of excavation is the need for thorough documentation. In industrial archaeology, documentation takes on added importance as it helps in understanding the function and historical context of the site. Techniques such as photography, mapping, and the creation of detailed records are crucial for capturing the site's layout, architecture, and machinery. This documentation process not only aids in analysis but also helps in reconstructing the site digitally, allowing for virtual exploration and preservation.

Another key consideration in industrial excavation is the use of stratigraphy. Stratigraphy involves analyzing the layers of soil and debris to determine the chronological order of their deposition. By carefully excavating each layer and recording its contents, archaeologists can unravel the timeline of industrial activity, identify changes over time, and gain insights into the social and economic conditions of the period.

Excavation strategies in industrial archaeology often involve a combination of mechanical and manual methods. While mechanical tools like excavators and bulldozers can help clear larger areas efficiently, delicate artifacts and structures require careful hand excavation. Students must be trained in both approaches to ensure the optimal balance between speed and accuracy.

Furthermore, safety precautions are of utmost importance when excavating industrial sites due to potential hazards such as toxic substances, unstable structures, or hidden underground utilities. Adequate protective gear, such as gloves, masks, and goggles, is necessary to ensure the well-being of the excavation team.

In conclusion, excavation techniques and strategies are vital for students of archaeology venturing into the captivating realm of industrial archaeology. By understanding the importance of documentation, stratigraphy, and the careful balance between mechanical and manual excavation, students will be well-prepared to uncover the hidden stories of the industrial landscape. Remember, safety is paramount in this field, so always prioritize the well-being of the team while unearthing the secrets of the past.

Documentation and Preservation of Industrial Heritage

In the field of archaeology, the study of industrial heritage is a fascinating and important area of research. As students of archaeology, it is crucial for you to understand the significance of documenting and preserving industrial heritage sites. Industrial archaeology allows us to gain insights into the development and transformation of societies through the lens of their industrial activities.

Documentation is the first step in preserving industrial heritage. It involves the systematic recording of sites, structures, and artifacts associated with industrial processes. This process helps us understand the historical context of these sites and their contribution to the growth of industries. Documentation can be achieved through various methods such as surveying, mapping, photography, and written descriptions. By creating a comprehensive record, we ensure that future generations can study and appreciate the richness of industrial heritage.

Preservation of industrial heritage is equally important. Once a site is documented, steps must be taken to protect it from decay, destruction, or inappropriate development. Industrial heritage sites often face numerous challenges, such as urbanization, lack of funding, and changing societal values. As students of archaeology, you can play a crucial role in advocating for the preservation of these sites.

There are several approaches to preserving industrial heritage. One method is through adaptive reuse, where old industrial buildings are transformed into new uses while still maintaining their historical character. This approach not only preserves the physical structures but also keeps the memory of industrial activities alive. Another approach is the establishment of industrial heritage parks or museums, where artifacts and machinery are displayed, and the history of industrial processes is interpreted for visitors.

Preservation also involves the conservation of artifacts and structures. This can be achieved through careful maintenance, repairs, and appropriate storage conditions. It is essential to involve experts in conservation and restoration to ensure the long-term preservation of industrial heritage.

As students of archaeology, you have the opportunity to contribute to the documentation and preservation of industrial heritage. By conducting research, participating in fieldwork, and engaging with local communities, you can help raise awareness about the importance of industrial heritage and advocate for its protection.

In conclusion, the documentation and preservation of industrial heritage is a critical aspect of archaeology. By documenting these sites and structures, we can understand their historical significance and contribution to society. Preservation ensures that future generations can appreciate and learn from these industrial landscapes. As students of archaeology, you have the power to make a difference by advocating for the protection and conservation of industrial heritage.

Interpreting Industrial Artefacts and Structures

In the vast realm of archaeology, industrial archaeology stands out as a fascinating and unique field of study. As students delving into this captivating subject, it is crucial to understand the methods and techniques involved in interpreting industrial artefacts and structures. This subchapter aims to equip you with the essential knowledge needed to unravel the secrets of the industrial landscape.

Industrial artefacts and structures are tangible remnants of the past, providing valuable insights into the development and transformation of societies. From towering factory chimneys to intricate machinery, these objects tell stories of innovation, labor, and technological advancements. However, interpreting these artefacts requires more than just a basic understanding of archaeology.

One of the key aspects of interpreting industrial artefacts is contextual analysis. By studying the historical, social, and economic context in which these objects were used, we can gain a deeper understanding of their significance. By examining archival documents, photographs, and oral histories, we can piece together the story of a particular artefact or structure and its place within the industrial landscape.

To further enhance our interpretation, it is important to investigate the technological aspects of these artefacts. Understanding the mechanics, materials, and processes involved in their production can offer valuable insights into the industrial processes of the past. This can be achieved through studying technical manuals, consulting experts in the field, and conducting scientific analysis.

Another crucial aspect to consider when interpreting industrial artefacts and structures is their spatial relationship. The arrangement of buildings, machinery, and transportation systems within an industrial site can reveal patterns of organization and workflow. By examining maps, blueprints, and conducting on-site surveys, we can gain a better understanding of how these structures functioned within their environment.

Furthermore, interdisciplinary approaches are highly beneficial in interpreting industrial artefacts. Drawing upon fields such as engineering, architecture, sociology, and history can provide a holistic understanding of the artefacts and structures we encounter. Collaborating with experts from these fields can enrich our interpretation and shed new light on the significance of industrial remains.

In conclusion, interpreting industrial artefacts and structures requires a multidimensional approach. By considering the historical context, technological aspects, spatial relationships, and embracing interdisciplinary collaboration, we can uncover the stories behind these remnants of the past. As students of industrial archaeology, this subchapter serves as a foundational guide to navigate the complexities of interpreting industrial artefacts and structures, allowing us to unlock the secrets of the industrial landscape.

Chapter 4: Types of Industrial Sites

Factories and Manufacturing Complexes

In the fascinating world of industrial archaeology, factories and manufacturing complexes hold a special place. These structures played a crucial role in the industrial revolution and continue to shape our modern society. In this subchapter, we will delve into the intriguing history and significance of factories and manufacturing complexes, exploring the different aspects that make them an integral part of industrial archaeology.

Factories and manufacturing complexes are physical manifestations of industrialization and technological advancements. They represent the transition from manual labor to mechanized production, marking a pivotal point in human history. These buildings, with their imposing facades and towering chimneys, stand as testaments to the ingenuity and progress of our ancestors.

One key aspect of factories and manufacturing complexes is their architecture. These structures were designed to facilitate efficient production processes while accommodating large machinery and the workforce. The architectural features, such as high ceilings, expansive windows, and open floor plans, were essential for natural lighting and ventilation, improving working conditions for laborers.

Moreover, factories and manufacturing complexes were often located near transportation routes, such as rivers or railways, to facilitate the movement of raw materials and finished products. This strategic positioning allowed for easy access to resources and markets, enabling industries to thrive and expand.

When exploring these sites, archaeologists uncover a wealth of information about the social and economic aspects of the time. The remains of machinery, tools, and infrastructure provide valuable insights into the manufacturing processes, revealing the technological advancements of the era. Additionally, artifacts found on-site, such as worker badges or personal items, shed light on the lives of the laborers who toiled within these walls.

The study of factories and manufacturing complexes also highlights the environmental impact of industrialization. The presence of pollution-control measures, such as smokestacks and water treatment systems, reflects the growing awareness of the consequences of industrial activities on the environment. By analyzing these features, archaeologists can trace the development of environmental regulations and their impact on industrial practices.

Understanding factories and manufacturing complexes is crucial not only for industrial archaeologists but also for anyone interested in the evolution of society and technology. By studying these sites, we gain a deeper appreciation for the laborers who shaped our industrial landscape and the impact of industrialization on our world today.

In conclusion, factories and manufacturing complexes are significant elements of industrial archaeology. Their architecture, location, and artifacts provide valuable insights into the technological, social, and environmental aspects of the time. By exploring these sites, students of archaeology can gain a deeper understanding of our industrial heritage and its impact on our modern world.

Mines, Quarries, and Extractive Industries

Mining, quarries, and extractive industries have played a pivotal role in shaping the industrial landscape throughout history. These industries have not only provided valuable resources for human civilization but have also left behind a rich archaeological legacy that sheds light on the progress of societies through time. In this subchapter, we will explore the significance of mines, quarries, and extractive industries and their contribution to industrial archaeology.

Mining is the process of extracting valuable minerals or other geological materials from the earth. From ancient times to the present day, mining has been an essential activity for human survival and economic development. Students of archaeology can uncover remnants of mining activities such as tools, infrastructure, and even the living conditions of miners, providing insights into the technologies and social structures of past civilizations.

Quarries, on the other hand, are sites where large quantities of stone, clay, or other materials are extracted. These materials have been crucial for building construction, sculpture, and pottery. By studying ancient quarries, archaeology students can learn about the techniques employed by ancient craftsmen, the transportation of materials, and the economic networks that existed for the distribution of these resources.

Extractive industries encompass a broader category that includes the extraction of various natural resources, such as oil, gas, and minerals. These industries have revolutionized the world and have fueled the industrial revolution. Archaeological investigations into extractive industries can reveal the impact of these activities on the environment, the technologies utilized, and the social implications of resource extraction.

Understanding the industrial landscape created by mines, quarries, and extractive industries is essential for students of archaeology. It allows us to comprehend the intricate relationship between humans and their environment throughout history. Such knowledge is invaluable for interpreting the past and informing present-day decisions regarding resource management and sustainable development.

In conclusion, the subchapter "Mines, Quarries, and Extractive Industries" delves into the significance of these industries in shaping the industrial landscape. It highlights the contributions of mining, quarrying, and extractive industries to the development of civilizations and provides insights into the technologies, social structures, and environmental impact of these activities. By studying these aspects, students of archaeology can gain a deeper understanding of the past and contribute to the sustainable future of resource utilization.

Transportation Infrastructure: Canals, Railways, and Ports

Transportation infrastructure played a pivotal role in the development of the industrial landscape during the 18th and 19th centuries. Canals, railways, and ports were crucial in facilitating the movement of goods, people, and ideas, effectively transforming the social and economic fabric of society. In this subchapter, we will delve into the significance of these transportation systems and their impact on industrial archaeology.

Canals were the first major transportation infrastructure developed during the Industrial Revolution. They offered a cost-effective and efficient means of transporting heavy goods over long distances. Students of archaeology will find canals fascinating, as they provide valuable insights into the engineering ingenuity of the time. The construction of canals required the excavation of vast amounts of earth, the building of locks and bridges, and the creation of reservoirs. By examining the remains of canals, students can uncover the technological advancements and social changes brought about by this transportation system.

The rise of railways in the mid-19th century revolutionized transportation. Railways not only enabled the rapid movement of goods and people but also spurred industrialization by promoting the growth of factories and industries along their routes. Archaeological exploration of railway infrastructure offers a unique perspective on the impact of this transportation system. Students can study the remains of railway tracks, stations, and signaling systems to understand the technological innovations that facilitated the emergence of this transformative mode of transportation.

Ports served as vital gateways for international trade and played a crucial role in the industrial landscape. As centers of economic activity, ports attracted diverse populations, resulting in the development of vibrant port towns. Archaeological investigations of port infrastructure provide valuable insights into the social and economic dynamics of these maritime hubs. Students can examine the remains of wharves, warehouses, and shipyards to uncover the complexities of trade networks and the global connections that emerged during the industrial era.

By studying the transportation infrastructure of canals, railways, and ports, students can gain a comprehensive understanding of the industrial landscape. These systems not only transformed the movement of goods but also shaped the social, economic, and cultural aspects of societies. Through the lens of archaeology, students can explore the technological advancements, social changes, and economic impacts brought about by these transportation networks. The subchapter on transportation infrastructure offers an exciting opportunity for students of archaeology to delve into the fascinating world of industrial archaeology and discover the hidden stories of the past.

Power Generation and Distribution Facilities

In the modern world, electricity is an essential part of our daily lives. We rely on it for lighting, heating, transportation, communication, and countless other activities. However, have you ever wondered about the origins of the power that fuels our society? This subchapter will explore power generation and distribution facilities, shedding light on the fascinating world of industrial archaeology.

Power generation facilities are the heart of our electricity supply system. These facilities convert various energy sources into electricity, which is then distributed to homes, businesses, and industries. The types of power generation facilities vary, depending on the energy source they utilize. Some common types of power generation facilities include hydroelectric plants, thermal power plants, nuclear power plants, and renewable energy facilities such as wind farms and solar power plants.

Hydroelectric plants harness the power of flowing water to generate electricity. They typically consist of a dam, which creates a reservoir, and turbines that convert the energy of the flowing water into electricity. Thermal power plants, on the other hand, use fossil fuels like coal, oil, or natural gas to generate heat, which in turn produces steam that drives turbines. Nuclear power plants generate electricity through a process called nuclear fission, where the energy released from splitting atoms is converted into electricity. Renewable energy facilities, such as wind farms and solar power plants, harvest energy from the wind and sun respectively, providing a more sustainable and environmentally friendly alternative.

Once electricity is generated, it needs to be distributed to consumers through an intricate network of power lines and substations. Power distribution facilities include transformers, which step up or step down the voltage of electricity to ensure safe and efficient transmission, as well as switchgear and circuit breakers to control the flow of electricity and protect the system from overloads.

Studying power generation and distribution facilities can provide valuable insights into the development of our industrial landscape. Archaeologists can uncover the historical evolution of power generation technologies, from early watermills to modern wind turbines. They can also examine the social and economic impacts of these facilities on local communities, as well as the environmental consequences of different energy sources.

By delving into the world of power generation and distribution facilities, archaeology students can gain a deeper understanding of the technological, social, and environmental forces that have shaped our modern world.

Chapter 5: Case Studies in Industrial Archaeology

The Iron and Steel Industry: Case Study of a Blast Furnace

In the vast realm of industrial archaeology, one cannot overlook the significant impact of the iron and steel industry. This subchapter delves into the fascinating world of blast furnaces, providing a detailed case study that unravels the inner workings of this crucial component of the iron and steel manufacturing process.

Blast furnaces are colossal structures that have played a pivotal role in shaping the modern industrial landscape. They are enormous, cylindrical structures made of refractory bricks, lined with ceramic materials capable of withstanding extreme temperatures. These furnaces are the heart of iron and steel production, where iron ore is transformed into molten iron, which is later processed into steel.

To understand the functioning of a blast furnace, it is imperative to explore its various components and processes. This subchapter will take you on a virtual tour of a blast furnace, beginning with the charging of raw materials such as iron ore, limestone, and coke into the furnace. The intense heat generated by the combustion of coke melts the iron ore, resulting in the formation of liquid iron known as pig iron.

Throughout this case study, we will explore the intricate mechanisms involved in the extraction of impurities from the molten iron, including the use of fluxes and the vital role of the blast of air injected into the furnace. The by-products generated during this process, such as slag and gases, will also be examined in detail, shedding light on their significance and potential applications.

Furthermore, this subchapter will shed light on the historical development of blast furnaces, tracing their origins back to ancient civilizations and highlighting their evolution over time. It will also explore the social and economic impact of blast furnaces on communities, emphasizing the pivotal role they played in the growth of industrial towns and cities.

By engaging with this case study, students will gain a comprehensive understanding of the iron and steel industry, its historical significance, and the technological advancements that have shaped it. They will also appreciate the interdisciplinary nature of industrial archaeology, as it combines elements of history, engineering, and material science to unravel the secrets of the past.

Overall, this subchapter serves as a gateway into the captivating world of blast furnaces, offering students a unique opportunity to explore the iron and steel industry from an archaeological perspective.

Textile Mills: Examining the Cotton Industry

The cotton industry played a significant role in shaping the industrial landscape of many countries, including the United Kingdom and the United States, during the 18th and 19th centuries. Textile mills were the heart of this industry, transforming raw cotton into a variety of textiles that were essential for the growing economies of the time. In this subchapter, we will delve into the fascinating world of textile mills and explore the impact they had on society and the environment.

To understand the cotton industry, we must first examine the significance of textile mills. These mills were large-scale factories that housed the intricate machinery required for processing cotton. Students of archaeology can gain valuable insights into this industry by studying the remains of these mills, such as the buildings, machinery, and associated artifacts. By examining these physical traces, we can uncover the technological advancements, labor conditions, and social dynamics that defined the cotton industry.

One of the key aspects to explore is the technological innovations introduced in textile mills. Students will learn about the development of machines like the spinning jenny and the power loom, which revolutionized the production process. These inventions led to increased efficiency and productivity, but they also brought about significant changes in the working conditions for laborers. By examining the machinery and understanding how it was operated, students can gain a deeper understanding of the industrial revolution and its impact on society.

In addition to studying the machinery, it is crucial to examine the social and environmental consequences of the cotton industry. By delving into historical records, students can uncover the living and working conditions of mill workers, including the long hours, low wages, and child labor that characterized this era. Furthermore, the environmental impact of textile mills cannot be overlooked. The pollution caused by the mills, such as the release of effluents into nearby water bodies, had detrimental effects on the surrounding ecosystems.

By examining the cotton industry through the lens of industrial archaeology, students can gain a comprehensive understanding of its significance and the complexities it entailed. This subchapter will provide a foundation for further exploration of the industrial landscape, encouraging students to dive deeper into the field of archaeology and its relevance to understanding our industrial past.

In conclusion, textile mills played a crucial role in the cotton industry, shaping the industrial landscape and having a profound impact on society and the environment. By examining the remains of these mills, students can uncover valuable insights into the technological advancements, labor conditions, and social dynamics of the time. This subchapter will serve as a stepping stone for students interested in the field of industrial archaeology, providing them with a solid foundation to explore the intricate world of the cotton industry.

Coal Mining and Collieries: Uncovering the Miners' World

Welcome to the fascinating subchapter on coal mining and collieries! In this section, we will delve into the captivating world of miners and explore the significant role they played in shaping the industrial landscape. As budding archaeologists, it is essential to understand the historical context and the profound impact of coal mining on society.

Coal mining emerged as a crucial industry during the Industrial Revolution, providing the energy needed to power factories, steam engines, and locomotives. In this subchapter, we will uncover the physical remnants left behind by miners and explore the social and economic aspects intertwined with this profession.

We will begin by exploring the physical remains of collieries, the sites where coal was extracted. As archaeologists, we will analyze the infrastructure, such as mine shafts, tunnels, and ventilation systems, to understand the complex operations involved in mining. By studying these structures, we can gain insights into the technological advancements and the challenges faced by miners.

While uncovering the miners' world, it is crucial to acknowledge the immense risks they faced daily. We will delve into the dangers associated with coal mining, such as cave-ins, floods, and the constant threat of gas explosions. By understanding these risks, we can appreciate the bravery and resilience of the miners who toiled deep underground.

Beyond the physical remains, we will explore the social aspects of coal mining. We will discuss the living conditions of miners and their families, including the development of mining communities and the establishment of colliery villages. By examining the artifacts and documents left behind, we can gain insights into the daily lives, struggles, and triumphs of these mining communities.

Furthermore, we will analyze the economic impact of coal mining, examining the distribution of wealth, the rise of mining corporations, and the exploitation of labor. By understanding the economic forces at play, we can comprehend the larger socio-political landscape during the Industrial Revolution.

This subchapter aims to provide you, as students of archaeology, with a comprehensive introduction to coal mining and collieries. By exploring the physical remains, social dynamics, and economic factors, we can gain a holistic understanding of the miners' world and its significance in shaping the industrial landscape.

So, grab your tools, put on your metaphorical mining helmets, and let's dive into the captivating world of coal mining and collieries!

Industrial Landscapes of the Industrial Revolution: Manchester and Birmingham

The Industrial Revolution, one of the most transformative periods in human history, brought about significant changes in society, economy, and technology. Two cities that played a pivotal role in this revolution were Manchester and Birmingham. In this subchapter, we will explore the industrial landscapes of these cities and delve into the archaeology behind their industrial heritage.

Manchester, often referred to as the "Cottonopolis," became the center of the cotton industry during the Industrial Revolution. The city's landscape was transformed by a network of canals, railways, and factories that sprouted up to meet the growing demand for cotton goods. Students of archaeology will find Manchester's industrial past fascinating, as they uncover remnants of mills, warehouses, and worker housing that tell the story of the city's industrial heritage. Excavations in Manchester have revealed the remnants of steam engines, spinning mules, and other machinery, providing valuable insights into the technological advancements of the time.

Birmingham, known as the "Workshop of the World," was a hub of manufacturing and metalworking industries during the Industrial Revolution. The city's landscape was dotted with foundries, factories, and workshops, all contributing to the production of goods such as guns, jewelry, and steam engines. Students studying industrial archaeology will have the opportunity to explore the remains of these industrial sites, uncovering the techniques and processes used during this period. Birmingham's canals and railway lines also played a crucial role in transporting goods, and their remnants offer a glimpse into the transportation infrastructure of the time.

By studying the industrial landscapes of Manchester and Birmingham, students can gain a deeper understanding of the social, economic, and technological changes brought about by the Industrial Revolution. The archaeological remains found in these cities provide a tangible link to the past, allowing us to explore the lives of workers, the impact of industrialization on the environment, and the development of new technologies. Through fieldwork, documentation, and analysis, students can contribute to our knowledge of these industrial landscapes and help preserve their historical significance.

In conclusion, the industrial landscapes of Manchester and Birmingham offer a rich tapestry for students of archaeology to explore. By studying these sites and artifacts, students can unravel the complexities of the Industrial Revolution, gaining insights into the lives of workers and the technological advancements that shaped the modern world. The preservation and understanding of these industrial landscapes are vital in recognizing the importance of our industrial heritage and its impact on society today.

Chapter 6: Industrial Archaeology and Urban Development

Industrial Heritage and Urban Regeneration

As students of archaeology, it is crucial to understand the significance of industrial heritage and its role in urban regeneration. The industrial landscape holds a wealth of historical and cultural value, telling the story of human progress and innovation. This subchapter aims to introduce you to the concept of industrial heritage and how it can contribute to the revitalization of urban spaces.

Industrial heritage refers to the physical remains and structures associated with industrial activities of the past. These include factories, mills, warehouses, canals, and other industrial infrastructure. These remnants offer valuable insights into the social, economic, and technological aspects of a bygone era. By studying these artifacts, we can gain a deeper understanding of the lives of those who worked in these industries and the impact they had on the development of cities and societies.

Urban regeneration, on the other hand, is the process of revitalizing and repurposing urban areas to meet the changing needs of the community. It involves breathing new life into neglected or abandoned industrial sites, transforming them into vibrant cultural, residential, or commercial spaces. Industrial heritage plays a crucial role in this process, as it provides a unique sense of identity and character to the regenerated areas.

When considering urban regeneration, it is essential to strike a balance between preserving the heritage value of industrial sites and adapting them to modern requirements. Industrial buildings and structures can be repurposed as museums, art galleries, community centers, or even as spaces for innovative start-ups. By incorporating these historical elements into the urban fabric, we create a sense of continuity and preserve the collective memory of the past.

Moreover, industrial heritage can have a positive economic impact on urban areas. Regenerated industrial sites often attract tourists, businesses, and investors, thereby boosting local economies. The preservation and adaptive reuse of industrial heritage can contribute to job creation, cultural tourism, and the overall improvement of the quality of life for residents.

In conclusion, industrial heritage holds immense value for archaeology students and the broader community. Understanding the significance of industrial heritage and its role in urban regeneration allows us to appreciate the historical legacy embedded in our cities. By actively preserving and repurposing industrial sites, we can create vibrant, sustainable, and culturally rich urban spaces for generations to come.

Challenges and Opportunities in Preserving Industrial Sites in Urban Areas

As students of archaeology, it is important to understand the challenges and opportunities that arise when it comes to preserving industrial sites in urban areas. The industrial landscape is a significant part of our history and heritage, showcasing the advancements and transformations that occurred during the industrial revolution. However, these sites often face numerous obstacles in their preservation.

One of the major challenges is the rapid urban development taking place in many cities. As urban areas expand, industrial sites are often seen as prime real estate for commercial or residential purposes. The demand for land and the economic benefits associated with redevelopment can overshadow the historical value of these sites. This results in the demolition or alteration of industrial structures, leading to the loss of tangible evidence of our industrial past.

Another challenge is the deterioration and decay of industrial sites over time. Many of these sites were not built with long-term preservation in mind, and the materials used may not withstand the test of time. Exposure to weather conditions, pollution, and neglect further contribute to their deterioration. Without timely intervention, these sites can become irreparably damaged, making their preservation even more challenging.

Financial constraints also pose a significant challenge. Preserving industrial sites requires substantial resources for maintenance, restoration, and interpretation. Limited funding often hampers the efforts to preserve these sites, as governments and organizations may prioritize other areas of heritage conservation. This creates a need for innovative funding strategies and partnerships between the public and private sectors to ensure the long-term preservation of industrial sites.

Despite these challenges, there are also opportunities to preserve industrial sites in urban areas. One such opportunity is the adaptive reuse of these sites. Repurposing industrial buildings for contemporary uses, such as cultural centers, museums, or creative spaces, can breathe new life into these structures while preserving their historical significance. This not only helps in their preservation but also contributes to the revitalization of urban areas.

Engaging with local communities and raising awareness about the historical and cultural value of industrial sites is another opportunity for preservation. By fostering a sense of ownership and pride among the community, there is a higher likelihood of support for their preservation and inclusion in urban planning.

In conclusion, preserving industrial sites in urban areas is a complex task that requires addressing various challenges. However, with careful planning, innovative strategies, and community involvement, these challenges can be overcome. As students of archaeology, it is our responsibility to advocate for the preservation of industrial sites and ensure that our industrial heritage is not lost to urban development.

Adaptive Reuse of Industrial Structures

In the ever-changing landscape of industrial archaeology, the concept of adaptive reuse has gained significant attention in recent years. As students of archaeology, it is essential to understand the importance and potential of repurposing industrial structures for contemporary use. This subchapter delves into the concept of adaptive reuse, exploring its significance and potential challenges.

Adaptive reuse refers to the process of taking an existing industrial structure and transforming it into a new functional space, while preserving its historical and architectural value. The practice has gained popularity due to its economic, environmental, and cultural benefits. By repurposing industrial structures, we can breathe new life into these remnants of our industrial past, creating sustainable and vibrant spaces that serve the needs of the present.

One of the key advantages of adaptive reuse is its positive impact on the environment. By utilizing existing structures, we reduce the need for new construction, minimizing the consumption of raw materials and energy. Moreover, adaptive reuse can contribute to the preservation of cultural heritage, as it allows for the retention of historical buildings that hold significant value to the community. By adapting these structures to new uses, we ensure their continued existence and appreciation for generations to come.

However, the process of adaptive reuse is not without its challenges. Students must be aware of the potential issues that may arise during the transformation of industrial structures. Structural integrity, zoning and building codes, and financial constraints are just a few of the factors that need to be carefully considered. Furthermore, striking a balance between preserving the historical character of the structure and creating a functional space can be a complex endeavor. Understanding these challenges is crucial for successful adaptive reuse projects.

To fully grasp the concept of adaptive reuse, students should also explore notable examples from around the world. From converted warehouses serving as trendy art galleries to former factories transformed into innovative office spaces, these examples demonstrate the endless possibilities of adaptive reuse. By examining these case studies, students can gain valuable insights into the creative and practical aspects of repurposing industrial structures.

In conclusion, adaptive reuse of industrial structures holds immense potential for archaeology students. This subchapter serves as an introduction to this fascinating concept, highlighting its significance, benefits, and challenges. By embracing adaptive reuse, we can contribute to the sustainable development of our industrial landscapes while preserving their historical and cultural value for future generations.

Industrial Archaeology as a Tool for Sustainable Development

In the world of archaeology, there is a fascinating field known as industrial archaeology. Unlike traditional archaeology that focuses on ancient civilizations and their artifacts, industrial archaeology examines the remains of more recent human activity, particularly from the industrial revolution onwards. This subchapter will explore how industrial archaeology can be a valuable tool for sustainable development, offering students an opportunity to dive into this niche of archaeology.

One of the key aspects of sustainable development is understanding the impact of human activity on the environment. By studying the remains of industrial sites, students can gain insights into the historical environmental practices and their consequences. For example, exploring the remnants of factories and mines can reveal the types of energy sources used, the waste disposal methods employed, and the impact on local ecosystems. Armed with this knowledge, students can better understand the long-term consequences of industrialization and develop strategies for more sustainable practices in the future.

Furthermore, industrial archaeology can shed light on the social and economic aspects of sustainable development. By examining the layout of industrial sites, the living conditions of workers, and the labor practices, students can gain a deeper understanding of the social inequalities and challenges faced by workers during the industrial revolution. This knowledge can inform discussions on fair labor practices, workers' rights, and the importance of social justice in sustainable development efforts.

Moreover, industrial archaeology provides a platform for exploring adaptive reuse and heritage conservation. As industrial sites become obsolete, there is often a debate about whether to demolish or repurpose them. Through careful study and analysis, students can propose innovative ideas for repurposing industrial sites in a sustainable manner. This could involve transforming old factories into cultural centers, converting disused railway lines into green spaces, or reimagining abandoned mines as heritage tourism destinations. By incorporating sustainable practices into adaptive reuse projects, students can contribute to the preservation of industrial heritage while also promoting sustainable development.

In conclusion, industrial archaeology offers students a unique perspective on sustainable development by examining the historical impact of human activity on the environment, society, and economy. By studying industrial sites and artifacts, students can gain insights into past practices and use this knowledge to inform present and future sustainable development efforts. Industrial archaeology provides a valuable tool for students interested in archaeology and sustainability, allowing them to contribute towards a more sustainable and equitable future.

Chapter 7: Industrial Archaeology and Environmental Impact

Environmental Consequences of Industrialization

Industrialization is a pivotal turning point in human history, marking the transition from an agrarian society to one driven by mass production and technological advancements. While industrialization has undoubtedly brought numerous benefits, it has also had significant and often detrimental consequences for the environment. In this subchapter, we will explore the environmental impacts of industrialization and shed light on the importance of industrial archaeology in understanding and mitigating these consequences.

One of the most prominent consequences of industrialization is pollution. The rapid growth of industries has led to the release of harmful pollutants into the air, water, and soil. Factories and power plants emit vast amounts of greenhouse gases, contributing to climate change and global warming. Additionally, the discharge of industrial waste into rivers and oceans has led to water pollution, affecting aquatic ecosystems and posing risks to human health.

Another consequence of industrialization is the destruction of natural habitats. As industries expand, forests are cleared, wetlands drained, and landscapes altered to make way for factory buildings, roads, and infrastructure. This destruction disrupts the delicate balance of ecosystems, leading to the displacement and extinction of numerous plant and animal species.

Furthermore, industrialization has had a profound impact on the quality of life for communities living near industrial areas. The exposure to toxic chemicals and pollutants has resulted in increased rates of respiratory diseases, cancers, and other health issues. Noise and light pollution from factories and machinery have also disrupted the sleep patterns and wellbeing of nearby residents.

Industrial archaeology plays a crucial role in uncovering the environmental consequences of industrialization. By studying the remnants of past industries, archaeologists can gain insights into the technologies and practices that caused environmental degradation. This knowledge can then be used to develop strategies for mitigating the negative impacts of present-day industries.

Moreover, industrial archaeology provides valuable lessons about the importance of sustainable development. By examining the mistakes of the past, students of archaeology can become advocates for environmentally responsible industrial practices. They can influence policy-making, raise awareness, and promote the adoption of cleaner technologies and sustainable approaches in modern industries.

In conclusion, industrialization has undeniably transformed the world, but it has also left behind a trail of environmental consequences. From pollution to habitat destruction and health issues, the impacts of industrialization are far-reaching. However, through the lens of industrial archaeology, students can gain a deeper understanding of these consequences and work towards a more sustainable future. By learning from the mistakes of the past, they can shape the industries of the future in a way that minimizes harm to the environment and promotes the wellbeing of both human and natural communities.

Pollution and its Legacy in Industrial Landscapes

In the realm of industrial archaeology, one cannot overlook the significant impact that pollution has had on the landscapes shaped by human industry. Pollution, in its various forms, has left a lasting legacy on the environment, raising important questions about the sustainability and long-term consequences of industrial development. This subchapter aims to delve into the intricate relationship between pollution and industrial landscapes, shedding light on the challenges faced by archaeologists when studying these sites.

Industrial landscapes are marked by the presence of factories, mines, mills, and other industrial structures that have shaped the development of societies over the centuries. These sites often bear witness to the environmental price paid for economic progress. From the early days of the Industrial Revolution to modern times, pollution has been an inherent byproduct of industrial activities. Whether it be air pollution from coal-fired power plants, water pollution from chemical spills, or soil contamination from industrial waste, the impact on the environment has been substantial.

Archaeologists studying industrial landscapes face numerous challenges. The physical remnants left behind by industries may contain hazardous materials, making excavation and exploration a delicate process. Furthermore, the effects of pollution can extend beyond the lifespan of the industry itself, requiring long-term monitoring and remediation efforts to mitigate the environmental damage caused.

Understanding the legacy of pollution in industrial landscapes is crucial for students of archaeology. By examining these sites, students can gain insights into the social, economic, and environmental implications of industrialization. They can explore the complex relationship between human activity and the natural world, as well as the ethical considerations surrounding industrial development.

Moreover, studying pollution and its legacy in industrial landscapes provides an opportunity for students to engage with contemporary environmental issues. By examining historical examples of pollution and its consequences, students can draw parallels to current debates on sustainable development, climate change, and the role of industry in shaping our future.

In conclusion, pollution has left a lasting legacy on industrial landscapes, shaping not only physical structures but also the social and environmental fabric of societies. The study of pollution in industrial archaeology is essential for students as they seek to understand the complexities of human-industry interactions and the long-term consequences of industrialization. By engaging with this topic, students can contribute to ongoing discussions on sustainability, environmental conservation, and the responsible use of natural resources.

Remediation and Restoration of Contaminated Industrial Sites

In the field of industrial archaeology, the study and preservation of contaminated industrial sites play a crucial role. These sites, often left abandoned or neglected after their industrial use, can pose significant environmental and health risks if not addressed properly. This subchapter will explore the importance of remediation and restoration of contaminated industrial sites, highlighting the methods used and the impact on archaeological research.

Remediation refers to the process of cleaning up and removing pollutants from contaminated sites, while restoration involves returning the site to a safe and functional state. These activities are essential for protecting both the environment and human health, as well as for preserving the historical significance of these sites.

When it comes to remediation, various techniques are employed depending on the type and extent of contamination. These can range from simple soil excavation and removal to more complex methods like bioremediation, which uses microorganisms to break down pollutants. The choice of remediation method should consider both the effectiveness of the technique and the preservation of archaeological features that might be present at the site.

Restoration, on the other hand, involves rehabilitating the site to ensure it is safe for public use while preserving its historical industrial character. This can include repairing or reconstructing buildings, infrastructure, and landscape elements. Balancing the restoration process with archaeological research can be challenging, as some elements may need to be removed or altered to ensure public safety, while others must be carefully protected to retain historical integrity.

For students of archaeology, understanding the remediation and restoration processes is crucial for engaging with industrial sites. These sites are not only valuable for their historical significance but also serve as important educational resources. By studying the processes of remediation and restoration, students can gain insights into the complexities of managing and preserving industrial heritage.

Moreover, the field of industrial archaeology can contribute valuable knowledge and expertise to remediation and restoration projects. Archaeological surveys and investigations can provide insights into the historical use of the site, identifying potential sources of contamination and guiding remediation efforts. This interdisciplinary approach ensures that the remediation and restoration of contaminated industrial sites are conducted in a holistic manner, considering both environmental and historical aspects.

In conclusion, remediation and restoration of contaminated industrial sites are critical for both environmental protection and historical preservation. By understanding the methods used and the challenges involved, students of archaeology can contribute to the conservation of industrial heritage, while also promoting sustainable practices. The integration of archaeological research in remediation and restoration projects ensures that these sites are not only cleaned up but also valued for their historical significance.

Balancing Conservation and Environmental Concerns in Industrial Archaeology

Industrial archaeology is a fascinating field that allows students to explore the remnants of past industrial activities and gain insights into our rich historical heritage. However, as we delve into the study of industrial sites and structures, it becomes crucial to strike a balance between conservation efforts and environmental concerns.

Conservation in industrial archaeology involves preserving and safeguarding the physical remains of industrial sites, buildings, and machinery. These artifacts provide valuable information about past processes, technology, and socio-economic conditions. They are tangible links to our industrial past and contribute to our understanding of how societies have evolved over time.

However, industrial archaeologists must also consider the environmental impact of their work. Many industrial sites, especially those associated with heavy industries like mining, manufacturing, or chemical production, may have left behind significant amounts of pollutants or hazardous materials. Excavations or restoration efforts can potentially disturb these contaminants, posing risks to both human health and the environment.

To address these concerns, it is essential for students of industrial archaeology to be aware of the potential environmental hazards associated with specific sites. Conducting thorough environmental assessments before undertaking any excavation or restoration activities is vital. This will help identify potential risks and develop appropriate strategies to mitigate them, ensuring the safety of both the archaeological team and the surrounding community.

Additionally, students should be well-versed in best practices for environmental management and remediation techniques. This includes implementing measures to prevent the spread of pollutants during excavation, using protective gear to minimize personal exposure, and employing specialized techniques for the safe handling and disposal of hazardous materials.

Furthermore, students should explore the concept of sustainable industrial archaeology, which aims to minimize environmental impacts while preserving and interpreting industrial heritage. This approach emphasizes the importance of considering alternative restoration methods that are environmentally friendly, such as using low-impact construction materials or implementing renewable energy solutions on-site.

By balancing conservation efforts with environmental concerns, students of industrial archaeology can contribute to uncovering and preserving our industrial heritage while safeguarding the environment for future generations. Understanding the potential risks and implementing sustainable practices will allow us to enjoy the educational and cultural benefits of industrial archaeology while minimizing any negative impact on our surroundings.

Chapter 8: Industrial Archaeology and Cultural Identity

Industrial Archaeology as a Cultural Resource

The field of Industrial Archaeology offers students a unique opportunity to explore the rich history and cultural significance of the industrial landscape. As a subchapter in the book "Discovering the Industrial Landscape: An Introduction to Industrial Archaeology for Students," this section aims to highlight the importance of Industrial Archaeology as a valuable cultural resource.

Industrial Archaeology focuses on the study and interpretation of the physical remains and artifacts related to industrial activities of the past. By investigating and analyzing these remnants, students gain a deeper understanding of the social, economic, and technological developments that have shaped our modern world. This subchapter aims to inspire students to explore the industrial heritage around them and to recognize its cultural value.

One of the key aspects of Industrial Archaeology is its interdisciplinary nature, drawing on various fields such as archaeology, history, engineering, architecture, and anthropology. Students can benefit from this interdisciplinary approach as it allows them to develop a holistic understanding of the industrial landscape. By studying the physical infrastructure, machinery, and industrial sites, students can uncover the stories of the people, communities, and industries that once thrived in these areas.

Industrial Archaeology also provides valuable insights into the impact of industrialization on society and the environment. Students can explore how industrialization transformed cities, landscapes, and even the lives of individuals. They can study the effects of industrial pollution, urbanization, and the development of new technologies on local communities. By understanding the past, students can contribute to current debates on sustainability, conservation, and urban planning.

Furthermore, Industrial Archaeology offers students the opportunity to engage in hands-on fieldwork and research. They can participate in excavations, surveys, and documentation of industrial sites, gaining practical skills and experience in the process. This hands-on approach allows students to connect theory with practice, enhancing their learning experience and fostering a deeper appreciation for the industrial heritage.

In conclusion, Industrial Archaeology is a fascinating field that uncovers the hidden stories of our industrial past. As students of archaeology, this subchapter encourages you to explore the industrial landscape as a cultural resource. By studying the physical remains and artifacts, engaging in interdisciplinary research, and participating in fieldwork, you can gain a deeper understanding of the social, economic, and technological developments that have shaped our world. Industrial Archaeology is not only a valuable academic pursuit but also a means to preserve and celebrate our industrial heritage for future generations.

Industrial Heritage and Identity Formation

In the ever-evolving world of archaeology, one area that has gained significant attention and relevance is industrial archaeology. This subchapter titled "Industrial Heritage and Identity Formation" delves into the fascinating connection between industrial heritage and the formation of identity. Targeted towards students with an interest in archaeology, this chapter aims to provide an introduction to the subject while highlighting its significance in understanding our past.

Industrial heritage refers to the physical remnants of industrial processes and activities that have shaped our societies. These remnants can include factories, mines, railways, canals, and other structures that were integral to the industrial revolution. Exploring industrial heritage allows us to uncover the stories of laborers, entrepreneurs, and communities that played a vital role in shaping the world we live in today.

One of the key aspects discussed in this subchapter is the relationship between industrial heritage and identity formation. Industrialization brought about significant changes in social, economic, and cultural aspects of life. As cities grew, new communities emerged, and with them, a sense of identity rooted in industrial activities. By studying the remnants of industrial landscapes, archaeologists can gain insights into how these communities formed and evolved over time.

Furthermore, industrial heritage can play a crucial role in preserving cultural identity. Many communities around the world have strong ties to their industrial past, and their heritage serves as a reminder of their achievements, struggles, and collective memories. Through the preservation and interpretation of industrial sites, archaeologists can help communities reconnect with their history and foster a sense of pride in their industrial heritage.

This subchapter also delves into the challenges faced in preserving industrial heritage. Rapid urbanization and economic progress often lead to the destruction of industrial sites, eroding the tangible links to our past. The importance of documentation, conservation, and public engagement is emphasized to ensure the survival of these significant landmarks.

In conclusion, "Industrial Heritage and Identity Formation" explores the profound impact of industrialization on our societies and the role of industrial archaeology in uncovering and preserving this heritage. The subchapter serves as an introduction for students interested in archaeology, offering insights into the importance of industrial heritage in understanding our past and shaping our collective identity. Through the exploration of industrial landscapes, archaeologists can not only uncover hidden stories but also help communities forge a stronger connection with their history.

Community Engagement and Public Interpretation of Industrial Sites

In the field of archaeology, industrial sites hold a unique place in our understanding of human history and development. These sites, once bustling with activity and innovation, now stand as a testament to the industrial revolution and the progress made in various sectors. However, the preservation and interpretation of these sites present a significant challenge. This subchapter aims to explore the importance of community engagement and public interpretation in industrial archaeology, particularly for students interested in this niche field.

Community engagement plays a crucial role in preserving and understanding industrial sites. These sites often have a profound impact on local communities, shaping their history, culture, and identity. By involving the community in the preservation and interpretation process, archaeologists can foster a sense of ownership and pride in these sites. Local knowledge and memories can provide valuable insights into the site's past, enhancing its historical significance.

Public interpretation of industrial sites is equally important. As students of archaeology, it is vital to communicate the significance of these sites to the general public. Public interpretation involves presenting the information in a way that is accessible, engaging, and educational. Interpretation methods such as signage, exhibits, guided tours, and digital media can help bring the stories of industrial sites to life.

Engaging the community and the public in industrial archaeology can have several benefits. Firstly, it can generate public support for the preservation and conservation of these sites, ensuring their long-term survival. Secondly, it allows for a broader understanding and appreciation of the technological advancements and societal changes brought about by the industrial revolution. Lastly, community engagement and public interpretation can inspire future generations to explore careers in archaeology and contribute to the field.

To effectively engage the community and the public, it is essential to employ inclusive and participatory approaches. Involving local stakeholders, such as residents, businesses, and heritage organizations, in decision-making processes can foster a sense of ownership and encourage collaboration. Additionally, utilizing digital platforms and interactive technologies can make the interpretation more accessible and engaging, especially for younger audiences.

In conclusion, community engagement and public interpretation are crucial aspects of industrial archaeology. By involving the community and effectively interpreting these sites, students of archaeology can contribute to the preservation, understanding, and appreciation of industrial heritage. As future professionals in this field, it is our responsibility to bridge the gap between academia and the public, ensuring that industrial sites remain an integral part of our cultural landscape.

Industrial Archaeology and Tourism

In recent years, industrial archaeology has gained increasing popularity among students and enthusiasts of archaeology. This subchapter aims to explore the fascinating intersection between industrial archaeology and tourism, highlighting the unique opportunities and challenges that arise when studying and preserving industrial heritage sites.

Industrial archaeology involves the study and interpretation of the material remains of industrial activities, such as factories, mines, railways, and mills. These sites, often abandoned or repurposed, provide valuable insights into the technological advancements, economic transformations, and social changes brought about by the Industrial Revolution and subsequent industrialization.

With the rise of heritage tourism, industrial archaeological sites have become important attractions for visitors seeking to understand the history and impact of industrialization. These sites offer a tangible connection to the past, allowing visitors to explore the physical remnants and experience the atmosphere of bygone industrial landscapes.

One of the key benefits of industrial archaeological tourism is its ability to stimulate local economies. By transforming former industrial sites into tourist destinations, communities can capitalize on their historical assets, attracting visitors and generating revenue. This, in turn, can lead to the revitalization of former industrial areas, creating jobs and fostering a sense of pride in local heritage.

However, industrial archaeological tourism also presents challenges. Preservation and conservation efforts must strike a delicate balance between safeguarding the integrity of the sites and making them accessible to the public. The structural decay and environmental degradation that often afflict industrial ruins require careful management to ensure their long-term survival.

Furthermore, interpretation and presentation play crucial roles in engaging visitors and conveying the significance of industrial heritage. Effective signage, exhibits, and guided tours can enhance the visitor experience, providing context and fostering a deeper understanding of the industrial past. Collaboration between archaeologists, historians, tourism experts, and local communities is essential to develop engaging narratives that capture the complexities of industrial heritage and its wider social, economic, and environmental implications.

In conclusion, the convergence of industrial archaeology and tourism offers unique opportunities for students and enthusiasts of archaeology. By exploring industrial sites, studying their material remains, and engaging with local communities, students can gain invaluable insights into the transformative impact of industrialization. Additionally, they can contribute to the preservation and promotion of industrial heritage, ensuring its appreciation by future generations. Industrial archaeological tourism not only provides educational and recreational experiences but also plays a vital role in economic development and heritage conservation.

Chapter 9: Future Directions in Industrial Archaeology

Emerging Technologies in Industrial Archaeology

As the field of archaeology continues to evolve, so do the tools and technologies that archaeologists use to uncover and understand the past. Industrial archaeology, a niche within the broader field, focuses on studying and interpreting the material remains of industrial processes and landscapes. In recent years, there have been exciting advancements in technology that have greatly enhanced the practice of industrial archaeology, allowing students and professionals to delve deeper into the industrial past.

One of the most significant emerging technologies in industrial archaeology is LiDAR (Light Detection and Ranging). This remote sensing method uses laser pulses to measure distances and create detailed 3D models of the Earth's surface. LiDAR has proven to be invaluable in uncovering and mapping industrial sites that may be hidden beneath dense vegetation or obscured by modern development. By using LiDAR data, archaeologists can identify and study features such as old industrial buildings, transportation networks, and even traces of long-abandoned industrial processes.

Another exciting development is the use of drones in industrial archaeology. Drones equipped with high-resolution cameras and LiDAR sensors can capture detailed aerial images and create accurate topographic maps of industrial sites. This technology allows archaeologists to survey large areas quickly and efficiently, providing a broader understanding of the industrial landscape. Drones also enable archaeologists to access hard-to-reach or dangerous areas, such as abandoned mines or industrial structures in remote locations.

Advancements in 3D scanning and modeling have also revolutionized the study of industrial archaeology. With handheld 3D scanners, archaeologists can capture highly detailed digital replicas of artifacts, structures, and entire industrial sites. These digital models can be used for analysis, virtual reconstructions, and even immersive virtual reality experiences, allowing students to explore and interact with industrial landscapes that no longer exist.

Furthermore, the application of Geographic Information Systems (GIS) has become an essential tool in industrial archaeology. GIS allows archaeologists to integrate various types of spatial data, such as maps, satellite images, LiDAR data, and survey data, into a single digital platform. By overlaying and analyzing these different layers of information, students can gain a more comprehensive understanding of the historical context, spatial relationships, and patterns of industrial sites.

In conclusion, the emergence of new technologies in industrial archaeology has opened up exciting possibilities for students in the field of archaeology. LiDAR, drones, 3D scanning, and GIS have all contributed to a more accurate and detailed exploration of the industrial landscape. These technologies enable students to uncover hidden industrial sites, survey vast areas efficiently, create immersive virtual experiences, and analyze data more effectively. As technology continues to advance, industrial archaeology will undoubtedly continue to benefit from these emerging tools, providing students with a rich and dynamic field of study.

Advances in Industrial Heritage Management

Industrial heritage management has witnessed several significant advancements in recent years, as professionals in the field strive to preserve and interpret the rich history of our industrial past. These developments have been driven by a growing recognition of the importance of industrial archaeology and a desire to engage with the diverse audiences, including students, who are interested in this field.

One of the key innovations in industrial heritage management is the use of technology. Digital tools and techniques have revolutionized how industrial sites are surveyed, documented, and presented to the public. High-resolution 3D scanning and drone photography allow for detailed and accurate records of industrial structures, ensuring their preservation even in the face of decay or demolition. These digital records also serve as a valuable resource for researchers and students, providing a virtual window into the past.

Another major advancement is the increased emphasis on community engagement and participation. Industrial heritage sites are no longer seen as isolated relics of the past but rather as valuable assets that can contribute to the social and economic development of their surrounding communities. This shift has led to the establishment of partnerships between heritage organizations, local authorities, and community groups, fostering a sense of ownership and pride in these sites. Students in the field of archaeology can play a crucial role in these initiatives, working alongside communities to uncover and interpret the stories of industrial heritage.

Furthermore, there has been a growing recognition of the need for sustainable management practices in industrial heritage sites. With a focus on conservation, restoration, and adaptive reuse, professionals strive to strike a balance between preserving the authentic character of these sites and ensuring their viability in the present and future. Students studying archaeology can explore innovative approaches to sustainable management, such as incorporating renewable energy sources or integrating industrial sites into broader cultural and educational programs.

In conclusion, the field of industrial heritage management has seen remarkable progress in recent years, driven by technological advancements, community engagement, and sustainable practices. These developments offer exciting opportunities for students in archaeology to contribute to the preservation and interpretation of our industrial past. By embracing these advances, students can actively participate in shaping the future of industrial heritage management and making this fascinating field accessible to a wider audience.

Collaborative Approaches in Industrial Archaeology Research

In the field of industrial archaeology, collaboration plays a vital role in uncovering and understanding the stories of our industrial past. This subchapter explores the various collaborative approaches that students in the field of archaeology can take to enhance their research and contribute to a deeper understanding of the industrial landscape.

Industrial archaeology research often requires interdisciplinary collaboration. Students studying archaeology can benefit greatly from partnering with professionals in fields such as engineering, architecture, history, and geography. By pooling together their expertise, students can gain a more comprehensive understanding of the industrial processes, technologies, and societal impacts that shaped our modern world.

One collaborative approach that can be particularly fruitful is engaging with local communities and organizations. Industrial sites are often deeply rooted in the social fabric of their surrounding communities, and involving community members in research projects can provide valuable insights and personal stories that might otherwise be overlooked. Students can organize community workshops, oral history interviews, or even collaborative fieldwork projects where local residents actively participate in archaeological excavations. By involving the community in the research process, students not only gain valuable knowledge but also foster a sense of ownership and appreciation for their cultural heritage.

Another collaborative approach is partnering with museums and heritage organizations. These institutions often have extensive collections, archives, and resources related to industrial history. Students can work with curators, archivists, and educators to access and analyze these materials, conduct research, and contribute to exhibitions and educational programs. Collaborating with museums also provides students with the opportunity to share their findings with a wider audience, fostering public engagement and raising awareness about the significance of industrial heritage.

Furthermore, collaboration can extend beyond traditional academic settings. Students can participate in online forums, join professional organizations, and attend conferences and workshops to connect with fellow researchers and practitioners in the field of industrial archaeology. These networking opportunities allow students to exchange ideas, share experiences, and collaborate on research projects, strengthening the overall knowledge base in the discipline.

In conclusion, collaborative approaches in industrial archaeology research play a crucial role in enhancing students' understanding of the industrial landscape. By engaging with various stakeholders, including local communities, museums, and fellow researchers, students can gain a more holistic perspective on industrial heritage. Collaborative research not only enriches their learning experience but also contributes to the preservation and interpretation of our industrial past for future generations.

The Role of Students in Shaping the Future of Industrial Archaeology

As students of archaeology, you hold a crucial role in shaping the future of industrial archaeology. The field of industrial archaeology explores the physical remains of past industrial activities and their impact on society. It is an interdisciplinary field that combines elements of history, archaeology, engineering, and architecture. By studying and understanding the industrial past, we can gain insights into the development of societies, technological advancements, and the impact of industry on the environment.

Your involvement in industrial archaeology can contribute to preserving and interpreting our industrial heritage. As students, you bring fresh perspectives, enthusiasm, and a passion for uncovering hidden stories. You have the opportunity to explore industrial sites, analyze artifacts, and document historical records. Your work can help shed light on forgotten industries, marginalized communities, and the lives of the workers who built the foundations of our modern world.

One of the key roles students can play in shaping the future of industrial archaeology is through research. By conducting original research projects, you can contribute to the existing knowledge and challenge existing narratives. Your research can focus on specific industries, regions, or even individual sites. It can involve archival research, fieldwork, and laboratory analysis. By conducting rigorous research, you can provide new insights into the development and impact of past industrial activities.

Another way students can shape the future of industrial archaeology is through community engagement. Industrial sites are often embedded in local communities, and their preservation and interpretation should involve the people who live in those areas. By engaging with local communities, you can build relationships, raise awareness, and foster a sense of pride in their industrial heritage. You can organize public lectures, workshops, and guided tours to share your knowledge and encourage public participation in industrial archaeology.

Furthermore, students can contribute to the development of innovative methods and technologies in industrial archaeology. With advancements in technology, there are new tools and techniques available for studying and documenting industrial sites. As students, you have the opportunity to experiment with these technologies and explore their potential applications in industrial archaeology. This can include 3D scanning, drone mapping, virtual reality, and data visualization. By embracing these technologies, you can enhance the accuracy and accessibility of industrial archaeological research.

In conclusion, students of archaeology have a significant role to play in shaping the future of industrial archaeology. Through research, community engagement, and the adoption of innovative methods, you can contribute to preserving our industrial heritage and understanding the impact of past industries. Your enthusiasm and dedication will ensure that the stories of our industrial past are not forgotten and that future generations can learn from and appreciate the legacy of industrialization.

Chapter 10: Conclusion

Recapitulation of Key Concepts and Themes

As we near the end of our journey through Discovering the Industrial Landscape: An Introduction to Industrial Archaeology for Students, it is important to take a moment to recapitulate the key concepts and themes we have explored throughout this book. By doing so, we can reinforce our understanding of the fascinating field of industrial archaeology and its significance in studying our industrial past.

First and foremost, we have learned that industrial archaeology is the study and interpretation of the physical remains of industrial activities from the past. These activities include factories, mills, mines, canals, and railways, among others. By examining these remnants, we gain valuable insights into the technological advancements, economic changes, and social impacts that accompanied the Industrial Revolution and subsequent industrial developments.

One of the central themes we have encountered is the relationship between humans and their environment. Industrialization transformed landscapes, often leaving behind scars on the natural world. Through our study of industrial archaeology, we have explored how these changes affected ecosystems, natural resources, and the overall balance between human needs and environmental preservation.

Another important concept we have delved into is the role of technology in shaping human societies. From the introduction of steam-powered machinery to the advent of mass production, industrialization revolutionized the way goods were produced and distributed, forever altering the course of human history. Through our examination of industrial sites and artifacts, we have gained a deeper understanding of the technological advancements that shaped societies and economies.

Furthermore, we have explored the social impact of industrialization. The rise of factories and mass production led to changes in labor practices, urbanization, and social stratification. By studying the physical remains of industrial sites, we can uncover the stories of the workers who toiled in these factories and mines, shedding light on their living and working conditions, as well as the social and cultural aspects of their lives.

In conclusion, Discovering the Industrial Landscape: An Introduction to Industrial Archaeology for Students has provided us with a comprehensive overview of the field of industrial archaeology. By recapitulating the key concepts and themes we have encountered throughout this book, we are equipped with a solid foundation for further exploration and research in the fascinating field of archaeological study. Whether you choose to pursue a career in archaeology or simply have a passion for understanding our industrial past, this book has laid the groundwork for a deeper appreciation of the industrial landscapes that surround us.

Implications and Significance of Industrial Archaeology for Students

Industrial archaeology is a fascinating field that offers students a unique opportunity to explore the material remains of our industrial past. This subchapter aims to shed light on the implications and significance of industrial archaeology for students, particularly those interested in the field of archaeology.

One of the most important implications of industrial archaeology for students is the ability to gain a deeper understanding of human history and technological advancements. By examining the physical remains of industrial sites, students can uncover the innovative techniques and machinery that revolutionized various industries. This knowledge not only provides insight into the past but also allows students to appreciate the progress made over time.

Furthermore, industrial archaeology enables students to develop crucial skills in research, data analysis, and interpretation. The field requires a multidisciplinary approach, combining elements of archaeology, history, engineering, and even environmental sciences. By engaging in industrial archaeological research, students can enhance their critical thinking abilities and learn to synthesize information from various sources.

Additionally, industrial archaeology offers students the opportunity to engage with local communities and contribute to heritage preservation. Many industrial sites are at risk of being lost due to urban development or neglect. Students can actively participate in surveying, documenting, and conserving industrial heritage, ensuring that future generations can learn from and appreciate these important remnants of the past.

The significance of industrial archaeology for students extends beyond academic pursuits. The skills acquired through studying industrial archaeology are highly transferable and can be applied to various career paths. Industries such as heritage management, museum curation, urban planning, and even engineering can greatly benefit from individuals with a background in industrial archaeology. Moreover, the ability to understand the historical context of industrial sites can contribute to more sustainable and informed decision-making in contemporary industrial practices.

In conclusion, industrial archaeology holds immense implications and significance for students interested in archaeology. It allows them to gain a deeper understanding of human history, develop valuable skills, contribute to heritage preservation, and pursue various career opportunities. By delving into the industrial landscape, students can uncover the hidden stories of our past and forge a path towards a more sustainable future.

Encouraging Further Exploration of Industrial Archaeology

As students of archaeology, you have embarked upon a fascinating journey of uncovering the hidden stories of our past. While traditional archaeology often focuses on ancient civilizations and historical sites, there is a whole world of exploration waiting for you in industrial archaeology. This subchapter aims to encourage you to delve further into this lesser-known field and discover the rich heritage of our industrial landscape.

Industrial archaeology is the study of the physical remains and structures associated with industry, such as factories, mills, mines, and transportation systems. It offers a unique perspective on the technological advancements, social changes, and economic developments that have shaped our modern world. By examining these remnants of our industrial past, you will gain insights into the lives of workers, the impact of industrialization on communities, and the evolution of our societies.

One of the reasons why industrial archaeology is particularly appealing to students is its hands-on nature. Unlike traditional archaeology, where artifacts are often fragile and require delicate handling, industrial archaeology allows for more interactive exploration. You can visit and explore old factory buildings, walk along disused railway lines, or descend into mines to experience firsthand the environments in which people once worked.

Furthermore, industrial archaeology offers a multidisciplinary approach, blending elements of history, engineering, architecture, and social sciences. This interdisciplinary nature allows students to develop a diverse skillset and gain a broader understanding of the past. By studying industrial archaeology, you will not only become proficient in excavation techniques but also develop skills in interpreting architectural plans, analyzing historical documents, and understanding the impact of industrialization on societies.

To further encourage your exploration, numerous resources and organizations cater specifically to the niche of industrial archaeology. Online databases, such as the Industrial Archaeology Database, provide a wealth of information on industrial heritage sites, allowing you to plan visits and conduct research. Additionally, societies like the Association for Industrial Archaeology organize conferences, workshops, and field trips, creating opportunities for networking and knowledge exchange.

In conclusion, industrial archaeology offers an exciting avenue for students of archaeology to broaden their horizons. By exploring the remnants of our industrial past, you will uncover the stories of workers, communities, and technological advancements that have shaped our modern world. The hands-on nature, multidisciplinary approach, and available resources make this field an excellent choice for students interested in delving deeper into the industrial landscape. So, put on your boots, grab your tools, and embark on an adventure to discover the hidden treasures of industrial archaeology.

www.ingramcontent.com/pod-product-compliance
Lightning Source LLC
LaVergne TN
LVHW020928200726
843506LV00011B/1881